I0788873

THE POWER OF SELF-BELIEF
"When No One Believes in You"

Marcia Wendt

Dedication

I dedicate this book to my beloved parents,

Amalani and Makalita (aka Finau) Tu'akalau, may your beautiful souls Rest in Peace.

Thank you for modeling the utmost strength, determination and work ethic towards serving the people of God. Thank you for loving and caring for me the best way you knew how. I know I haven't been the easiest child to raise but know, that I am so grateful for you both and for my trials, for I would not have discovered my fight in me.

I have realized you were both only trying to protect me, and I am forever thankful, but I have promised myself, I will not let those limitations stop me from creating what God has instilled inside of me. I Love and miss you both so much.

Forever your favorite child 😊 ha ha!

Table of Contents

Chapter 1: Unrecognizable

If someone were to tell me, one day I would become a Motivational Speaker, have the opportunity to travel and meet some of the most influential people on the planet, speak on stages and share my message with the world and become a Best-Selling Author,

I would say "You're Crazy" "You've got the wrong girl."

Because, what had been said over my life from a young age is hard to even imagine, the opportunities and the life I live now, could have been possible for someone like me. So, as I look back and see how far I've come, who I've had to become, and what I've had to overcome,

"Whoa!"

My life is barely recognizable!

I didn't have many people believe in me.

You see, I was that little girl, who failed most of her way through high school. I certainly wasn't one of the brightest or the smartest kids in class. I was a slow learner. Some teachers called it, 'A learning disability' and told me I needed to get myself checked.

I knew I wasn't learning as fast as the other students, and because of that I was also labelled 'dumb' by my math teacher.

"You're going to be nothing—a big fat Zero Marcia."

Sometimes she would say it in front of the class, so the other students could hear. I knew, if I didn't start laughing and brushing it off, like it didn't bother me, the students would laugh at me, so I laughed with them.

Eventually school work became very boring and I was getting frustrated because no matter how hard I'd try, I couldn't keep up with other students, so I took on the role of "the class clown" and "the naughty kid."

Yeah, that kid! The kid that was spoken about in the staff-room.

I realized I had lived up to those labels and believed it was part of who I was, however, I did have this innate feeling deep down inside of me that I wasn't "Dumb" or "Stupid." I had just been misunderstood.

The summer of 1990, High School had finally come to an end. Some students were excited about going to Uni or Tafe to further their education, some planned to work in their family business' and a few like myself, had no idea what we wanted to do, and I was okay with that. The day was an emotional day for us all. We had spent 4 years together, sharing some great moments and not so great moments, but we all knew it was never going to be the same.

On that evening, we had our Graduation Mass. We gathered together at my local parish church, St John of God, Auburn. Towards the end of the mass, it was time to receive our certificates. My Principle called out the names one by one and we were to walk towards the front of the altar where my Deputy Principal would greet us, congratulate us and hand out our Graduation Certificates.

"Marcia Tu'akalau" (maiden name) my Principle called. As I walked towards the altar with a smile, I thought to myself, *I'm so glad I got to graduate together with my friends. It may have not been the best result, but I'm relieved, it is finally over!*

As my Deputy Principal greeted me and reached out to shake my hand, handing me my Certificate, he looked straight at me with a smirk on his face and murmured, "Congratulations Marcia, I can't believe you made it".

It wasn't till moments after I had walked away that I realized what had been said. He caught me by surprise!

I guess some would say, 'Why would you be surprised Marcia? You failed most of your way through high school, that shouldn't have come as a surprise to you?'

I guess, hearing it from another person hurts more, than you believing it.

As I sat back down in my seat I remember wishing I had the chance to exchange a few words of my own, but being in the house of the Lord, I knew that wasn't going to happen.

After graduating school and working for a few big companies, it wasn't till then, in my adult years I had discovered I was dyslexic.

Being told by an old boss who I didn't quite see eye to eye with, whom I learnt it from.

But...we won't get into that story now. I'll leave that, for another time.

Discovering this made so much sense to me, as to why I had difficulties learning at school and felt like 'An outcast', but on the bright side, it has also given me a great understanding, to why I've been able to accomplish and prove certain things to my former employers, and to other people where I've been told "It couldn't happen" or "It's never been done before."

This book is not about the Teachers or the discovery of dyslexia or how I was raised as I will mention later in the book.

This book is about the combination of lessons I have learned through these circumstances and the life experiences I've had to overcome, that have shaped my life to who I am today and the power of self-belief I had to build within myself, when no-one believed in me. It's about how I saw the world differently and how it made me understand there is more to a person then what meets the eye.

Chapter 2: Black Sheep

I grew up in a very well respected family in Auburn in the inner western suburbs of Sydney, Australia. My parents were upstanding citizens of the St John of God Auburn Parish and the wider Tongan Community in Sydney. My mum was involved in many things, but I will name just a few. She was a JP (Justice of Peace - Judicial Officer), she had helped majority of the Tongan families migrate in to the country in the late 70's and early 80's, helped them find work and a place to stay. She was the chairperson for some of the community services in our local area and was known as 'Big Mama' to the local farmers and the shopkeepers.

We lived in a beautiful four-bedroom home with eleven people that my parents had bought and renovated back in the 80's. It was my mum, my dad, my aunty, my adopted little brother and seven girls including myself, me being the second youngest. We also had a granny flat at the backyard that was always occupied by either a family member or a friend of the family that my parents were helping out.

Although my parents did great deeds and it was illustrated to the community, at home, was a bit different. We were brought up in a very old fashioned, traditional way. My parents were very overprotective, my dad especially. I could understand why he would be that way (Like any dad) he had seven daughters to protect. He was protective, but he also became very violent with us if we stepped out of line.

My parents weren't affectionate, at all, neither were we, (Even if we tried, I don't think we'd know how to). Expressing one's feelings and being "Vulnerable" we were led to believe it was a sign of "Weakness", so that just became the norm in our household.

Like any other household, we had rules we had to abide by, some may differ depending on culture, value or beliefs.

In my case, asking questions on why things were done a certain way was a sign of disrespect and not expressing my opinion was considered "Being humble."

Some of these house rules were quite extreme, some would say, but we didn't know any better. Our home phone had it fit with a lock at the bottom of the phone, so no one other than my parents could use it unless it was an emergency. Having a social life outside of school or work was just out of the question. We weren't allowed to take part in any activities or sports outside of school. We weren't allowed to have friends over or go over to their houses. We had an all girl's family band, (*We did pretty well back in the days, must I add ☺*) that my older sister started up and that was to be our main focus. We were pressured to part take in the family business, regardless if we were musically talented or not, it was a must. We practiced almost every week night and travelled doing gigs every weekend, to church social nights to birthdays, weddings and new year parties, you name it.

Yeah, you could say, I felt betrayed. Robbed of my childhood. I felt I missed out on a lot of growing up and skipped straight to adulthood. I felt something was missing, like having a void inside or something, but I didn't know what.

After a while these rules became suffocating. I rebelled against these rules and would often bend reality to my desires.

I started to voice my opinion on certain things, not because I was undermining my parent's authority, but because I had a lively inquiring mind. I was very interested in everything and anything. But, to my parent's, I was being disrespectful, especially when none of my older sister's voiced their opinion.

My parents became very frustrated with me over the years and expressed it quite often (*Physically*) as I would have liked it. But I was persistent, (*Which didn't help*) and it eventually escalated into violent anger. My mum would yell at me to go outside and fetch the biggest and thickest stick I could find and bring it back to her so she could beat me with it till I was black and blue. It got so bad at times I couldn't wear my school uniform to school because the bruises were pretty bad, the teachers would often send me to after school detention, because I wouldn't tell them why.   After every beating, I would run and hide under my bed and cry silently so no one could hear me. I would often wonder if my mum and dad had ever cared about me or even loved me. I knew I didn't deserve this, but it left me as a very confused child.

Some days I would watch my sisters, to see if it bothered them and to be honest, it was hard to tell. I'm not sure if they were frightened to speak up or it really didn't bother them at all.

Eventually they turned their anger towards me and started to do exactly what mum and dad was doing, beat me and yell at me. They were frustrated because whenever mum and dad got angry at me, which meant mum and dad were in a bad mood for the next hour or two, they were also getting a mouthful from them at times.

"Why don't you shut your big mouth you little sh*t!" they would yell at me. "What's wrong with you?!"

Sometimes I was just sick and tired of hearing the same thing, I'd just shrug it off as if it didn't bother me, but it really did. It bothered me a lot to be honest, because I knew I didn't do anything wrong, but unfortunately, they all thought otherwise.

Here is a little exercise I'd like you to do...

I'd like you to write down when in your life you have experienced being "Misunderstood" by a loved one or someone at work and write down how it made you feel and what you did about it or if you didn't do anything about it and why?

____

____

____

____

____

____

Chapter 3: The Dance of Fear

Dancing: Oh boy, how I loved to dance!

When I discovered my love for dancing, it was the only thing I ever wanted to do for the rest of my life. I dreamt of becoming the world's best dancer. It was all I ever wanted.

Dancing was freedom to me. It was the freedom to express how I felt. Hearing the beat of the music allowed me to connect with my soul. It gave me the freedom to create my own identity, my uniqueness and be whoever I wanted to be. It gave me the freedom for my body to move in all different ways and it made me feel so free. At times I felt I was in a trans. My own trans.

Giving me that happy feeling deep down in my belly. *Oh, how I loved to dance!*

When no one was at home I would lock myself in my room and turn the volume up as loud as I could dancing around the room imagining I was performing on a stage in front of thousands of people.

I didn't have much interest in school work, except for an event our school participated in, a dance and drama event, 'The Rock Eisteddfod.'

It was a friendly competition between schools around the region, aimed to promote healthy lifestyle choices, particularly abstinence from drugs, alcohol and cigarettes.

I imagined myself auditioning, but I didn't have the self-belief and the confidence I needed, so I hid behind the "I'm too cool for this sh*t" story. I was lying to myself and others when I said that I had no interest. You see, no one at school knew I loved to dance, and no one knew I could dance, because I was too busy living up to other people's perceptions of me as the "Class clown" and "The naughty kid."

But that was all about to change.

My friend asked me to wait for her after school so we could walk home together, she was auditioning for one of the lead roles.

"Yeah sure, I'll just wait here" I said, and off she went.

I waited in the playground. An hour went by and I began to get bored.

I went looking around the school building where the audition was. I finally found it and I tried to peek into the classroom, but I couldn't see much. I decided to climb up onto the lockers to get a good look through the louvers. As I sat there quietly watching the audition, hoping I wouldn't get busted, I couldn't help myself, I started laughing out loud at one of the student's auditions (*Of course I did*).

Yes, I was that kid! And I'm not proud of it too.

I quickly ducked my head away from the louvers and tried to jump off the lockers as fast as I could, but it was too late.

The teacher rushed out of the classroom and scolded me for interrupting the audition, about how rude I was. This wasn't the first time I had heard this, and it wasn't going to be the last time either.

The teacher told me to follow her, so I did, not knowing what she was planning to do with me. We walked into the classroom and all the students were staring and giggling at me because I just got busted.

She stopped in front of the classroom and turned around to me and said, "Marcia, since you find this funny, you are going to dance for us."

"Excuse me Miss, What!?" trying not to choke on my words.

"Dance Marcia."

Is she serious? I thought to myself

"When you're ready." She persisted as she walked away towards her desk.

And before I knew it, the music came on, and I was still trying to figure out '*What in the world had just happened.*'

She stared at me, waiting for me to move or do something, but I couldn't. I couldn't move my feet. I wanted to run. But everyone's eyes were on me. I stood there frozen with terror. My palms were sweating and my armpits were dripping with sweat inside my school uniform and all hairs on my body standing on end.

It was that moment, I realized. I had just come face to face with my "Greatest fear."

My self-doubt, not believing in myself, the feeling of 'Not being good enough' and afraid of what people would say or think of me. I hadn't realized, the labels I had lived up to and attached myself to, had really affected me inside. And while everyone was staring at me waiting for me to do something, this is what was going through my mind.

Then, I heard a high-pitched voice from the back of the room,

"Is she just going to stand there?"

Then all of a sudden, something shifted inside of me and ignited this burning fire, my body automatically went into autopilot and I started to move to the beat of the music. I closed my eyes and I imagined I was back in my bedroom dancing like I was performing on that stage, I had always dreamt about. I was in my element. I felt free. I felt happy and I felt comfortable because I was doing what I loved to do to. And before I knew it, the song was over and I could hear the cheering and applauding from the students and an approved look on my teacher's face. From that day forth I was seen in a new light. I got the role and became popular among my peers and teachers, this time, for the right reasons.

"I learnt that courage was not the absence of fear, but the triumph over it. The brave man is not he who does not feel afraid, but he who conquers that fear." – Nelson Mandela.

Do not be afraid of your fears. For your fears are your friend. Its job is to show up in your life to develop parts within yourself you have not discovered yet, to live a happy life. The more you overcome what you are afraid of, the more life opens up. It is nothing more than an obstacle that stands in the way of your progress. So, embrace it, acknowledging it, and learn to dance with it.

We have all faced fear in some way or another in life. Write the very first time you had come face to face with your greatest fear? And how did you handle that situation or maybe you didn't, but if you were to know, how would you have handled it?

____

____

____

____

____

____

____

____

____

Chapter 4: You Gotta Stay Hungry

Fast forward to 2005, I was working casual as a cashier attendant for a German food store company. My husband and I were going through some financial hardship, so this casual job wasn't ideal, but it was better than nothing. I inquired about a full-time position as I desperately needed some income stability. Applicants needed managerial qualifications or at least some kind of experience to become an assistant manager or a store manager, and I had neither, but I was determined to change that.

A week into my job, I got promoted as a deputy, (Similar to a supervisor) but the only way I could benefit from it, was if both managers were off and I was managing the store, which was the occasional weekend.

As the weeks and the months went by. I kept bugging my store manager to give more hours on the weekend and persuaded her to go home earlier so I could close the store and get paid the extra rates as a deputy, and of course she was happy to take me up on my offer.

I admired her work ethic from afar and would watch how she managed her team and the whole store. She was tough and one of the best in the company and she inspired me.

Almost twelve months in the same position, she noticed I was hungry to learn more, and I wanted more. So, she took me under her wing and taught me everything she knew.

"You know, I'm going to be tough on you Marcia."

She said.

"Yeah, I know, it's okay. I'm tough too." I said sarcastically with a smile on my face, so eager for the new challenge, yet feared if I was way over my head.

Boy! She sure wasn't playing. She was tough!

I was a size AUS 14 at the time and I quickly shredded those pounds off in no time.

You see, I never had anyone believe in me like she did or even gave me a chance, and I respected her more for that.

After a few weeks of working with her, I was able to pick up more shifts more regularly this time.

One particular weekend I closed the store and I accidently forgot to send through the store orders to the suppliers for the next delivery. When I came to work the next day I was called into the manager's office. I didn't think anything of it, as it wasn't unusual for me to be in there, but this time was different. I walked in and saw her and the area manager (her boss) standing there, both looking at me. They greeted me as I walked in and then she walked out straight after, which started to concern me.

"Take a seat, Marcia."

"No, I'm good thank you. Is everything alright?"

I asked with a concerned look on my face.

As he sat down, he asked me about the orders. At first, I had no idea what he was talking about.

"The orders Marcia, you didn't send them. Why didn't you send them?"

I didn't respond right away as I was tracking back my steps from last night's closing. Then realized what I had done.

I had forgotten to send the orders.

I apologized profusely to him and ensured him it would never happen again, as I knew the effect it would have in the store. It was my first mistake, so I thought he would give me a verbal warning and let this pass.

But that wasn't the case. He skipped the whole disciplinary procedure and bluntly said,

"Maybe, Marcia you're not a fit for this position."

I was shocked and puzzled as to why he would be so harsh. I stood there quietly for a few seconds looking at him with this lump in my throat. Then I softly asked him if there was anything else.

"No, Marcia." he replied.

"Okay. Thank you." I said and walked out, as fast as I could without making it obvious, I wanted to cry. I was in disbelief at what had just taken place.

As soon as I shut the office door behind me, I practically ran into the staff toilets, and burst out in tears, quietly though. I didn't want him to hear me from the next room. I couldn't believe what he said. I had never been pulled up before and then to tell me "Maybe I'm not fit for this position." This played over and over in my mind and the more I did, the more it made me furious, questioning myself, *"Maybe he's right. Maybe I'm not."*

After crying it all out and getting all my frustrations out, I washed my face and looked straight at myself in the mirror and said

"Right! I'll show him. Marcia, you are not going to let him tell you what you can and what you can't do."

And that is exactly what I did!

I was promoted as an assistant manager not long after the incident than promoted as a store manager 7 months after both in the same year and became the first cashier assistant in the company to become a store manager within 2 years of employment.

A couple of years later, I bumped into him at a manager's meeting in head office, he looked shocked to see me and said

"Wow. You've come a long way Marcia."

I smiled politely, thanked him and kept walking.

Now, "I don't say this to impress you, but to impress upon you" – Les Brown

"The importance of believing in yourself when no one does is immeasurable, because when you believe in yourself you will become unstoppable."

Food for Thought:

When people don't believe in you, they don't believe in themselves. So rather than getting emotionally caught up in what had been said, learn to take full responsibility in becoming your own champion and work towards building your "Self - Belief" muscle and create the life or dream life you know you deserve.

Chapter 5: Sisterly Love

My younger sister has always had an amazing unique gift of turning nothing into something magical as an event stylist.

Since she was a little girl, she used to help mum set up tables for functions for the community. Ever since then, she has been the stylist for our family gatherings.

For many years, we encouraged her to start her own business, but she would always make excuses as to why she couldn't,

"Oh no! My kids are too young."

"Oh no! I'm just happy to style for only our family."

"Oh no. I wouldn't know where to start."

"Oh no! I'm happy just to stay home and support my husband and look after the kids."

It was one excuse after another (her bag of excuses, I called it) and to be honest, it was wearing me out. But she's my little sister, so I would put up with it, well... only for a little while. 😊

It was clear she lacked self-confidence, and self-belief within herself, but I saw great potential in her, we all did but she wasn't willing to do anything about it, and that saddened me.

So, one afternoon, I decided I had enough of her excuses and if she wasn't going to do anything about it, than I sure was. I gathered some photos of her finest work from previous work she had done and I posted it up on my personal/ business Facebook page and tagged as many people as I could, including her of course!

I then wrote a congratulations post on how she had finally decided to start-up her new business as an event stylist and was ready to share her gift with the world.

After about an hour, she called while I was at my hairdresser appointment. Without hesitation I picked up my phone to answer with a cheeky grin on my face and before I could say anything, I heard her laughing out loud and said,

"You bloody b*tch! OMG! What did you do?"

We didn't say much on the phone, other than, having a good laugh about the whole situation. I could tell she was still in shock and terrified at the same time. Like any sister, I gave her words of encouragement and told her "Everything was going to be okay." I told her she had nothing to worry about and that the family and I believed in her and that's all that mattered. I had tremendous faith in her.

She knew, from that point on there was no turning back and it was a choice of

'She either; sinks or she swims!' haha!

Fifteen months later, I'm so proud to say she has successfully styled for a setting of 400+ in one given time and has been hired by over 80 satisfied clients and is still growing.

Food for thought

Sometimes in life when we don't believe in ourselves, borrow other people's belief in us, till we work to build and strengthen our own belief in ourselves.

I want you to take a moment and think back to a time you wanted to accomplish something.

It could be anything big or small, and as much as you really wanted it, you backed out, you talked yourself out of it, you doubted yourself or became too concerned about other people's opinion of you or you believed you weren't good enough. Whatever the case, maybe I want you to ask yourself these questions and write your thoughts down;

a) **How would life look like for me today, if I didn't doubt myself, or if I believed I am good enough or if I wasn't so concerned about other people's perception of me?**

    ____

    ____

    ____

    ____

    ____

    ____

    ____

b) **Ok. What about 12 months from now? How would life look like for**

me right now. Even if I don't know,
but if I were to know. How would it
look?

____

____

____

____

____

____

____

c) And in 5 years' time?

____

____

____

____

____

____

____

Write your answers down before moving to the next question.

Let me ask you this, do you believe;

"If NOTHING has changed in the last 5 years, then NOTHING will change in the next 5 years."

Tick your answer.

Yes: _________

No: _________

Whether your answer is Yes or No. I want you to write, Why?

____

____

____

____

____

____

Chapter 6: Self Assess

I know in my life, I've missed out on a few opportunities that have passed me by because of the lack of confidence, the self-doubt and the limiting beliefs I had about myself.

I wish, I knew what I know now or if I knew sooner, how much of a difference it would make in my life.

Just imagine if you had an absolute unshakeable confidence in your ability to achieve anything you put your mind to?

What would you want to wish and hope for?

What would you dare to dream of, if you believed in yourself with such deep conviction that no matter what fears of failures you are going to face, you are going to achieve them?

What difference would it make in your life?

Because the ability to believe in yourself can change your life.

The famous Henry Ford says

"Whether you think you can, or you think you can't – you're right!"

Here's a few exercises I'd like you to take your time and write your answers down, don't rush.

1) I want you to close your eyes and think back to a time in your life where you last believed you could do anything you put your mind to? Either big or small. It could be riding a bike, driving a car, or a project you were working on and you thought you'd never accomplish it, yet you did or a promotion you thought you couldn't achieve, and you did?

   ____

   ____

   ____

   ____

   ____

2) What were, your thoughts, your feelings and your emotions at that time? Did you feel happy, proud, satisfied, motivated, unstoppable or fearless etc.

____

____

____

____

____

____

3) Now, I want you to ask yourself, what the difference is then and now. What have you done differently?

____

____

____

____

____

____

4) Has life shaped you in a way you have forgotten who you are? Or did someone talk about you in a negative way?

____

____

____

____

____

____

____

Make sure you write down your answers
to all questions before you move to the
next step.

Taking Action

5 Simple Steps

Keep in mind...Your results will determine the amount of action steps you take.

For instance:

If you study a book about "Learning how to ride a bike" but you haven't taken the action steps towards riding a bike then the information you have studied, is just knowledge, going nowhere.

If you study the book and implement the action steps and stay consistent, then it's only a matter of time that you will see the results of your work.

So, to develop your self-belief muscle here are some action steps for you to get started on today.

1. Write on your bedroom or bathroom mirror and repeat this to yourself 3 times a day.

I AM ENOUGH

I AM WORTHY

I AM DESERVING

I CAN BE WHOEVER I WANT TO BE

AND I BELIEVE IN ME

2. Refer to your answers on Chapter 3. Q3.

Now, I want you to go out or do something, (either big or small) you enjoy doing that will bring back that feeling of happiness,, unstoppable, feeling motivated or inspired and proud of yourself back into your life today.

I know for me, whenever I am in self-doubt, I write down all the things I've accomplished, which reminds myself how far I've come and say to myself, *"I will not allow anyone to steal my joy!"*

3. Write down a bucket list of the things you've always wanted to do, big or small.

E.g.: I know I've always wanted to ride on a Harley Davidson, and I know I will be soon 

Personal goals are great to start with. E.g.

"Growing up I've always wanted to learn

how to drive a manual and now I know how."

Your goals can be as small as that to start with, it is up to you.

Then tick them off as you go along.

4. Stretch yourself out of your comfort zone by doing something you've never done before at least once a week.

I know for me, my challenge at the moment is reading 3 books a month. I had never read a book ever, while I was at school.

Learn to not allow people to steal your joy. Surround yourself with people you can learn from, people who inspire you and people who will lift your spirit up.

"You are the average of the five people you surround yourself with."- Jim Rohn

So, choose wisely!

5. Lastly, my favourite , celebrate yourself for all your small wins, because any little progress each day, adds up to big results.

Before I go, I'm going to leave this with you...

"A bird sitting on a tree is never afraid of the branch breaking, because her trust is not on the branch but on her own wings." - Unknown

So, Trust and Believe in yourself because what you think you are looking for on the outside, is already inside of you and if someone like me can do it, so can you.